Praise for *Pommy Granita*:

"Clever, refreshingly original poems as an indictment of injustice, peppered with insightful, humorous comments on contemporary events."

—Emeritus Professor Stuart Rees AM,
poet and founder of Sydney Peace Foundation

"Insightful, powerful and refreshing."

—Jon Hill, Editor, *West England Bylines*

Praise for Jake Lynch's fiction:

"Fast-moving and fascinating, with a number of entertaining sub-plots ... convincingly recreated"

—Telegraph review of *Blood on the Stone:
An Oxford murder mystery of the 17th Century*

"Very enjoyable. Fast-moving and highly entertaining."

—Peter Tickler, author of the *Blood in Oxford* series

Accolades for Jake Lynch's work on Peace Journalism:

Winner, Luxembourg Peace Prize, 2017, for contributions to theory and practice; Book of the Conference, Conflict Research Society, 2014, for *A Global Standard for Reporting Conflict* (Routledge)

Praise for Jake Lynch's public advocacy from management at the University of Sydney:

"Inappropriate and naïve."

Jake Lynch is an Associate Professor in the University of Sydney Faculty of Arts and Social Sciences, where he teaches into the Masters of Social Justice.

His poetry has appeared in *Trad and Now*, *New Bush Telegraph* and *West England Bylines*.

Jake's debut novel, *Blood on the Stone*, an historical mystery thriller set in Oxford of the 17th Century, was originally published in e-book and paperback by Unbound Books. His own recording of the audio book was published in 2023. The *Oxford Mail* called it: "An absorbing and ultimately compelling read … a gripping narrative, based on well-rounded characters, in a convincingly recreated milieu of time and place."

In scholarly work, Jake is the most published and most cited author on Peace Journalism, with six books and over sixty articles and book chapters to his credit. For his contributions to both theory and practice, he was awarded the 2017 Luxembourg Peace Prize, by the Schengen Peace Foundation.

Before taking up an academic post, in 2007, Jake enjoyed a near-20-year career in journalism, with spells as a Political Correspondent for Sky News and Australia Correspondent for *The Independent*, culminating in a role as on-air presenter at BBC World TV News, where he presented over a thousand live half-hour news programmes. He won five international awards for his documentary film, *Soldiers of Peace*, narrated by Michael Douglas.

POMMY GRANITA

*Progressive comic verse for
Boundless Plains and Old Sod*

Jake Lynch

Insight Horizon Books

Published Insight Horizon Books
emdrinsight.com/insight-horizon-books

First published 2023

Copyright © Jake Lynch, 2023

The moral right of the author has been asserted.

All rights reserved. Without limiting the rights under copyright restricted above, no part of this publication may be reproduced, stored in or introduced into a retrieval system, or transmitted, in any form or by any means (electronic, mechanical, photocopying, recording or otherwise), without the prior written permission of the copyright owner and publisher of this book.

A catalogue record for this book is available from the National Library of Australia

ISBN 978 0 6458806 0 1 (pbk)
ISBN 978 0 6458806 1 8 (ebk)

Cover photo by Peter Boyle
Designed and typeset by Helen Christie, Blue Wren Books
Printed by Ingram Spark

To Annabel and Finn, as ever

Contents

Introduction   1

Boundless Plains

1. Three Kings   7
2. Net Zero or bust   12
3. Progressive comic haiku   13
4. Rime of the AUKUS Submariner   16
5. Budget Day   18
6. Al-Nakba Day   22
7. Assange Unbound   27
8. Greta and the garbos   30
9. Gadarene swine   33
10. Seeking asylum   36

Both and neither

1. Huskisson   41
2. The other side   45

Old Sod

1. Snapshots of Brexit   53
2. Britain in 2023   58
3. Getting to Yes in Wales   60
4. Lab or a Tory?   64
5. Ode: Intimations of Inveracity from Recollections of Labour Childhood   66

Notes   75

Introduction

Two occasions, the Professor reckoned,
When poetry saved the ruling class:
In 'twenty-six, as anarchy beckoned,
Then when Brixton's riot came to pass.
Both shook capitalism's foundation;
Lit fires that had to be extinguished.
The elixir, to unify the nation?
Send folk in to teach the buggers English!

By then we all were modernists, of course;
No more need for lines to scan or rhyme.
So Dylan Thomas told his aunt, recourse
To punctuation can be a crime.
Ah, but comic verse—now that's different, see;
As D, if still with us, would agree.
We can distance ourselves with irony
From literary hegemony.

So what's the novel angle, slant or twist
From this little volume in your hands?
To bring perspectives previously missed,
As from mob, being forced off their lands?
Listening to voices we've excluded
From publishing, academy or slam?
Don't let's be in any way deluded:
This poetry is just who I am.

Shaped by struggle and resistance, it's true—
Though generally at second hand;
Solidarity, the cause and issue
For speaking out and taking a stand.
Should we only read where we agree?
The converse is true in poetry:
We de-anthologised Ezra Pound
When we realised with whom he'd hung around.

Then, is 'free verse' all it's cracked up to be?
Seemingly the fashion and the trend;
Overland, as well as over sea,
As the *cognoscenti* will contend.
So here you'll find stuff serious, with jokes.
Which one of those is the verse itself?
That's in you, dear reader, to evoke—
Just don't leave it sitting on the shelf.

Notes and references

When I read English at Cardiff University, in turbulent 'Thatcher's Britain' of the 1980s, the Professor, Terry Hawkes, linked the very foundations of our study with the clashing social forces beyond the classroom. The official report on the 1981 inner-city 'riots', or uprisings, by a High Court judge, Lord Scarman, recommended instilling a sense of belonging to the existing order by promoting the study of humanities in general, and English in particular. Brixton—the iconic setting for the troubles—offered "outrageous symbolism", Hawkes wrote,[1] as the flames of riot licked around Shakespeare, Milton and Chaucer Roads in London SW2.

The prescribed remedy for the discontents revealed by the unrest echoed that of an earlier report, by senior civil servant Henry Newbolt, after the General Strike of 1926. A canonical notion of 'Eng Lit', as a repository of assumptions and values all could share, was supposed to bind the wounds of a society fracturing along lines of class and race, thus palliating demands for change from unionised workers and urban youth alike.

Spotter's corner: In *A Letter To My Aunt Discussing The Correct Approach To Modern Poetry*, Dylan Thomas warns specifically against the criminality of commas. The reference in "mob, being forced off their lands" is to *We Are Going*, title poem of the first published verse collection by an Aboriginal writer, Oodgeroo Noonuccal, in 1964. *Overland* magazine is probably Australia's most prolific publisher of original poetry, nearly all of it free verse, little or none meriting the term, 'comic'.

Boundless Plains

1. Three Kings

A King of Earth in godly realm arose
With lairy Queen Consort in pantyhose.
Wangaratta's Earl of Loudoun held spurs
Of gold and velvet (since you're wondering).
We don't know how Charlie's going to go
But he did concur when Kerr called Time, so …
We could raise a glass to remember Gough.
Now, it's the G-G who says when we're off
To war. So maybe things are getting worse.
Ever get that foreboding?

A King of Laughter dressed himself as she.
In younger days, he liked a drink or three.
A prize in his name—his global cachet
As Australia's cultural attaché—
Was given, then quashed; his prejudice deemed
Amiss, since gender was his comic theme.
And those he'd raised when he was strong; they, meek?
They fled from him, that sometime did him seek.
A new fashion of forsaking.

A King of Air inflamed the Trumpist horde.
A hate magnet for an audience, bored
With the Beltway, entitled, mad as hell;
Then, out-Foxed by malicious emails, fell.
Dominion won. Surprise! He came untucked.
Cost Murdoch, and you're seriously fucked.
Strangely, back in Blighty, a flame-haired Wade
Got away with it, dodged blame for phone-hack.
Harry sued, but the King called off the pack.
What can there be on him, besides gold braid?

No day off work for crowning old Jug-Ears.
Perhaps there'll be a long weekend next year.
Commemorative double demerits will apply.
Still, at least we got a Crown emoji
#Coronation—and a chocolate bust.
So pass the Duchy 'pon the left hand side.
If Waleses don't get it, Sussexes must.
Just never, ever mention Di, who died.

That thrice-anointed name: Chazza, Chas, Chuck.
The First one lost his head in dire defeat.
Second, restored, pretended to the feat
Of curing scrofula with regal touch.
A nominative-determinist augury of strife?
And will the subjects tolerate that second wife?

Baz got cred for "upending cultural cringe".
Away with lame, home-grown classical takes
('But soft—what wind in yonder dunny breaks?')
And begone with toffee-nosed pommy whinge.
He "brought an astringent and anarchic
Australian theatre to the world" instead.
"Goodnight Possums," his wondrous valedic-
tion: a part of him that'll never quite be dead.

Carlson's lies were legion and egregious,
Cutting down to size the wokerati;
Riling up confected racial grievance
To support the Elephantine Party.
But hold. Freedom for Assange was one of Tucker's issues.
Leaving Cuba to Cubans, another.
Maybe they're what got him into bother.
Commentators all lined up to diss you,
TC, but even tedious argument, of insidious intent
Can lead us to some interesting questions./

I can show you something different
from either your morning podcast talking beside you
Or your evening chatshow rising to meet you.
I can show you fear on a smartphone screen.

And breathe. No man is an island, Donne said
(He forgot the Isle of Man). Where to head
For some common theme in these threaded tales?
What hope create, before our courage fails?

Barry disaligned, Tucker realigned.
Shall we and CRIII prove misaligned?
One's passed, one's deposed and One's on the throne.
Might he be the last? Surely as we raise
Our Voice, we can speak for ourselves alone?
We can't all be Kings: there the problem lies.
An earth of living things holds us in embrace.
We belong to it, not contrariwise.
So let's seize this moment, stand tall before the sun
And start a new story, open to everyone.

Notes and references

Strange as it may seem, royal ladies are not allowed to display bare legs to the hoi polloi.[2] In warmer months, sheer pantyhose may be worn for public appearances—so Camilla, Queen Consort, probably did that at the Coronation.

Even stranger, there really is an Earl of Loudoun, and he really does live in the Victorian 'rural city' of Wangaratta. Simon Abney Hastings, the 15th of his line, even has a distant claim to the throne, it seems. Rather than press the point, he contented himself with carrying the 17th-Century Great Golden Spurs. "Their use in the coronation ritual derives directly from the ceremony of creating a knight," apparently.[3]

Correspondence from 1976, reported in Australia in 2020,[4] shows King (then Prince) Charles wrote to congratulate Governor-General John Kerr for sacking the Labor government of Gough Whitlam, three years after it won office on the famous campaign slogan, "It's Time". The report in March 2023 of the Inquiry into Australia's Entry into Overseas Conflict recommended restoring the role of 'Commander in Chief', under section 68 of the constitution; which would, in certain circumstances, mean the Governor-General deciding whether and when to go to war.[5]

The belief, popular from medieval times, that a laying-on of hands by the King could cure scrofula (inflamed swellings on the neck caused by a bacterial infection of the lymph nodes) features in *The King's Evil*, a fine mystery thriller by Andrew Taylor set in the 1670s.[6] It describes stricken subjects filing solemnly past Charles II to gain this tactile (though futile) privilege.

The King of Laughter, Barry Humphries, leant his name to a prize at the Melbourne Comedy Festival, which was then withdrawn after he made prejudiced comments about trans people. The appraisal of his contribution to Australian theatre comes from an obituary by his biographer, Anne Pender, in *The Conversation*.[7]

The King of Air, Tucker Carlson, was fired from his role as star presenter of Rupert Murdoch's Fox News after it settled a libel action by Dominion, a manufacturer of voting machines it had falsely accused of rigging the 2020 US presidential election. Carlson's emails, tendered in evidence, showed the network was well aware the allegations were unfounded; thus revealing 'malice', which extinguished Fox's First Amendment rights.

Spotter's corner: *Pass the Dutchie ('Pon the Left Hand Side)* was a chart hit for the British-Jamaican band, Musical Youth, in 1982. The tedious argument of insidious intent is from TS Eliot's *The Lovesong of J Alfred Prufrock*, and the italicised stanza that follows is a slightly changed (updated?) version of a section from *The Waste Land* (where fear is shown in a handful of dust). John Donne's poem from which the famous quote is taken is also called *No Man is an Island*.

2. Net Zero or bust

Is Robert Frost's wood still yellow with trees?
Do Banjo's parrots still call on the bough,
Or Wordsworth's daffodils nod in the breeze?
In Sunburnt Country, fire danger says 'low',
But rain builds fuel loads, which signboards don't show.
So as we alternately bail and broil,
How come we keep on prospecting for oil?
And what must we do to reach Net Zero?

Enjoy the Pastoral in lyric verse
But ask yourself what's better, and what's worse:
Inconvenience on the Harbour Bridge –
A road less travelled by, once in a while—
Or pandering to climate change denial;
Heating the planet while cooling the fridge?
Electric cars to take us to our camp
Or eternal dread of both drought and damp?

When Vi Coco looked on that tent of blue
Which prisoners call sky, it filled with fumes
From fossil fuels that dimmed its limpid space.
For there she was sent, by a bully-court,
With coppers desperate not to lose face.
Ah but, we heard, Violet was not our sort
Of person. Enter the Knitting Nannas,
Challenging draconian protest law—
For someone has to stop new coal and gas,
Lest Mackellar's beauty cede to terror.

We can't eat money, as more now discern;
One of these days, the politics will turn.
It's we who must force the point to its crux,
Through petitions and—yes—sometimes roadblocks,
Though it makes the four-wheel-drive owners cuss.
Else we'll find the payback will be on us:
The lavish plains and paddocks will stay dry,
Or drown beneath floodwater where they lie;
And that karmic ghost-dog from Gundagai
Turn out to have shat in our tuckerbox.

3. Progressive comic haiku

Extractivism
Will it meet its Waterloo
Over Beetaloo?

Notes and references

Climate activist Violet Coco was sentenced to 15 months' imprisonment for blocking one lane of the Sydney Harbour Bridge, for about half an hour, by parking a truck across it (the sentence was then overturned on appeal).[8]

Former Prime Minister Scott Morrison (who he?—Ed) disparaged electric cars as unsuitable to take people to a weekend camp.

The Environmental Defenders Office, a heavyweight legal NGO, took up a case against NSW anti-protest laws—which would shame many an authoritarian regime—brought by veteran environment advocates, the Knitting Nannas.[9]

Spotter's corner: Robert Frost set *The Road Less Travelled By* in a "yellow wood". The parrots call on the bough in Banjo Patterson's bush classic, *On The Trek*. William Wordsworth's daffodils fell upon that inner eye which is the bliss of solitude. For how long will the natural treasures celebrated in such verses remain in their present condition, amid a rapidly changing climate?

Dorothy Mackellar's *I Love A Sunburnt Country*, with its references to lavish plains and paddocks (which can turn to sources of terror in bushfire season) holds a similar iconic status in Australia. The tent of blue that prisoners call sky is from Oscar Wilde's *The Ballad of Reading Gaol*. Both he and Vi were arguably political prisoners.

The dog is in *Nine Miles from Gundagai*, by Jack Moses, in which a drover complains of mounting problems—the hostile weather, his cart's broken axle and so forth. Among all these, "the dog sat on the tuckerbox." A non-sequitur, surely? What, precisely, would be so troublesome in such a turn of events—especially in context of all the others? No, that is Moses' own version, sanitised for publication, of the words in the original folk song, where the dog *shat in* the tuckerbox.[10]

Among the (no doubt) many attractions of Gundagai, in southern New South Wales, is the Dog on the Tuckerbox Recreational Trail, which takes the visitor, on foot or by bike, to a stone plinth surmounted by a bronze statue of—sure enough—a dog sitting on a tuckerbox.

Haiku

Somehow, in 2023, the Northern Territory government arrived at the conclusion that it's a good idea to detonate a notorious 'carbon bomb' by allowing fracking for gas across the massive Beetaloo Basin. Along with its potentially disastrous consequences for the climate, it's yet another instance of Aboriginal communities being trampled roughshod in a shameless and heedless stampede for lucre.

If anyone will stop them, it did not, at time of writing, appear likely to be the federal government—despite its declarative commitments to limit global heating. As so often in such situations, the best hope seemed to reside with the grassroots campaign of protest getting underway, led in this case by the land's traditional owners.[11]

4. Rime of the AUKUS Submariner

The ocean is restless tonight.
Is that the surf on cliffs at Dover Heights,
Up, and back, unheeding?
Or melancholy, long, withdrawing roar
Of empire, receding?
Once, a fleeing General came ashore;
Took charge, returned as pledged, but then hove to.
Now wants us to gang up on you-know-who.
So should we keep old allyship afloat?
And must we really buy those bloody boats?

Here on Burning Deck, we've met disaster
Upon disaster: 'Nam, Afghan, Iraq.
When triumph comes, we'll treat that impostor
Just the same. (Shout, won't you, when one embarks.)
The menace and caress of waves obscure
A plot to dominate, submersible.
A wise philosopher once wrote that "power
Is most effective when least visible".

What kind of country do we want to be?
Broke, broke, broke on thy cold grey steel, O Sea?
Can't afford rent caps, "pixie dust" of youth;
Decent public welfare, or health?
So this must be democracy by stealth—
Where sands of hope are washed away, like truth.

Have we not moved on from Federation?
"Equality of man" did not apply
To China, Barton said. Maturation
Has surely brought a broader view. So why
Do we still seem so readily beguiled
By headlines sensationalist and wild?
Subs were never voted on in Caucus,
It appears. No wonder tides of contest
Are running high—with clear call, and raucous.
So let's all go, and join the peace protest.

Are we to be convinced we're under threat?
Think-tanks chivvy us to believe their lies.
An arms-trade-funded study? *Quelle surprise!*
It recommends we buy more fighting kit.
A *cri de coeur*, amid confused alarms
Of struggle and flight, gets you called *naïve*,
With multi-billions staked on taking arms
And *avantage* in hi-tech make-believe.
(A little Gallic *perspicacité*
To expose official *mendacité*.)

Pick sides, and one must win, the other lose.
Instead, sum a whole greater than the parts—
Work together, create a common boost:
Make an enemy? No, be counterparts.
We may now be choosing how our own story ends.
So think:
Do we swim together, or sink?
The ship we need is not of fools, but friends.

5. Budget Day

There once was a Treasurer, Jim,
Whose Budget went out on a limb
To buy submarines,
But neglected the means
Of people less wealthy than him.

When it came to projections of force,
There was plenty for weapons of course,
But rattling the tin
For power of wind
Was an item he wouldn't endorse.

The ostensible point of the scheme
Was protection from China's big dream,
But when they saw the plan
And arms for Japan
They complained "we're the mote—you're the beam!"

Opposition from both Red and Green
Was discounted as widely foreseen,
But if unions campaign
For the peace to sustain
We can turn back those deadly machines.

Notes and references

"Ostensible" is a key word in the debate over Australia's initiative to partner with the US and UK in ordering a fleet of nuclear-powered submarines, with an estimated price-tag of $368 billion. The *ostensible* aim of such a decision would be to acquire new military capability— but that was on its way from 2016 when Defence agreed the supply of diesel-powered vessels from France, at a fraction of the cost.

The political reputation of then-PM Morrison took another downward turn when he reneged on the deal. French President Emmanuel Macron was asked whether he thought Australia had acted deceitfully. His succinct reply—"I don't think: I know"—proved an instant hit. Hence the salutary effect of a dip into French, to expose official mendacity, in the closing section of the poem. Anthony Albanese, as Opposition leader, merely informed the parliamentary Labor Caucus the party was backing the new scheme, without putting it to a vote.

The *ostensible* purpose of the Virginia-class fleet is defensive, yet Alison Broinowski, a retired diplomat and President of Australians For War Powers Reform, drew attention to some strange wording in an official report that seemed to provide legal cover for Australia to go to war with China—again, on US coat-tails—over Taiwan.

The report in question was from the Inquiry into Australia's Entry into Overseas Conflict. It ignored the large majority of submissions calling for decision-making power to be vested in Parliament rather than the Executive. Instead, it proposed to restore the role of the Governor-General as Commander in Chief in "conflicts that are not supported by resolution by the United Nations Security Council, or an invitation of a sovereign nation given that complex matters of legality in public international law may arise in respect of an overseas commitment of that nature". As Broinowski pointed out,[12] a *non*-sovereign nation that might invite Australia to join a war could only be Taiwan.

The fleeing General was Pacific Allied Commander Douglas MacArthur, who left his HQ on the Philippine island of Corregidor in a hurry under Japanese advance in 1942 and found refuge in Australia. After victory three years later, he personally returned as pledged, but, in another sense, it marked the point when the US itself became the General. The submarine order coincided with a switch in military doctrine to be not merely 'interoperable' with the US but 'interchangeable'.

The 'China threat' thesis that drives Australia's arms build-up has, in turn, been driven by think-tanks such as the Australian Strategic Policy Institute, whose *ostensible* job is to "provide contestability in advice to ministers". So when official intelligence agencies reach a view—as they did when providing input to a Defence White Paper in 2009—that China's own military build-up is "purely defensive", it can be overruled in favour of a more severe assessment, thereby justifying more public money for the arms industry. That'll be the arms industry which is, in turn, a major sponsor of ASPI itself.

The Nine newspapers—traditionally broadsheets of record, the Melbourne *Age* and *Sydney Morning Herald*—grabbed attention from the rest of the media (and quite possibly perked up their mostly elderly readership) with headlines implying an imminent danger of attack from China. This was based *ostensibly* on strategic analysis, though historian Marilyn Lake highlighted its appeal to underlying tropes and prejudices: "The sensationalist propaganda-style image printed on the front page of our newspaper in which Chinese jet fighters depart Red Communist China heading straight for Australia, constitutes a shameless and shameful invocation of past racial fears and antagonisms that will do great harm."[13]

Spotter's corner: poetry with a maritime theme has often been seen as supplying imagery and invoking meanings to sustain reactionary, distinctively militaristic notions of Britain and its place in the world. Unsurprising, perhaps, for a traditional naval power—but that makes it a propitious field for the supply of new angles and directions, in efforts to undercut and subvert them. I do so, in *Rime of the AUKUS Submariner*, by addressing several such poems directly.

The opening stanza echoes that of Matthew Arnold's *Dover Beach*, with the onomatopoeic effect of alternate long and short lines mimicking the swash and backwash of waves. In the original, it is Anglican Christianity that is seen as receding, with a melancholy roar—making the poem a nostalgic hymn to a supposedly lost Tory realm: still a potent idea in British politics.

The boy who stood on the burning deck is valorised, in *Casabianca* by Felicia Dorothea Hemans, for remaining at his post (during the Battle of the Nile in 1798) much longer than was good for him. Rudyard Kipling's *If* is often name-checked as the all-time favourite poem of the British, with its exhortation to meet the twin impostors, Triumph and Disaster, just the same. The point is, following the US to war has led Australia into plenty of the latter, whereas the former has, for some time now, remained elusive.

The "menace and caress of waves" is from *The Dry Salvages*, one of TS Eliot's Four Quartets. The sociologist Steven Lukes gave us—in his influential 1974 essay, *Power: A Radical View*—the aphorism: "Power is at its most effective when it is least observable," offering an irresistible metaphorical link with submarines. Alfred, Lord Tennyson's original is, of course, "Break, break, break/On thy cold, grey stones, O sea."

Australia is far from broke, but Treasurer Jim Chalmers, having to squirrel away cash to begin paying for the submarines, pleaded poverty in the face of demands to do more in his Budget to support the living standards of the less well-off. (The notion of capping rents to benefit young tenants was dismissed in parliament by the Prime Minister as "pixie dust"). The ocean transmits "a wild call and a clear call" in John Masefield's *Sea Fever*.

6. Al-Nakba Day

We ate no citrus when I was a lad.
You could buy fascist oranges from Spain,
But the flavour would come with bitter taint.
Racist ones, from South Africa, the same.
We eschewed those, despite the TV ads,
Running with no apparent sense of shame.
That just left Jaffas, labelled 'from Israel'.
The one remaining case where justice failed.

Three quarters of a century now gone,
Of unimaginable loss and pain,
At least to us, with our privileged lives.
So let Mahmoud Darwish take the baton
To elevate our discourse, and explain
How the people feel and think, as they strive
For freedom, and to spend their days at home—
Not consigned to exile or forced to roam.

Not so fast. "I don't choose to represent
Anything except myself," he once wrote;
"But that self is full of collective memory."
Which brings us neatly to another quote:
"The metaphor of Palestine is stronger than
The Palestine of reality."
It's up to us to work out what he meant.
He learned and broke all words to make "homeland".

But how come we're involved, this far away?
The honest answers strain to scan or rhyme.
Impunity, extended over time;
Ignoring calls to use whatever sway
We have to force accountability.
Feigning to believe in a unicorn
'Peace process', as if birthright is forsworn,
Which makes us guilty of complicity.

Then it depends on who is meant by 'we'.
Sydney's last eyewitness of '48
Said the real Australian folk story
And his own were as one. This on The Date,
To a crowd outside Town Hall, with elders,
Present and emerging. A red and green
Striped Rabbitohs scarf warmed a dog they'd brought
In a shopping trolley. Two right colours
Out of three: not bad, they probably thought.
So, for al-Nakba Day, this was the scene.

Ideal weather, said a woman (quite glam):
Cool, but not too cold, with just enough breeze
To stir the flags. The tiger of Eelam,
Gold on blood; Left shades, different by degrees,
And iconic billowing tricolour
Of Mahmoud's enigmatic metaphor.

Later, café coffee, with madeleines
To stir remembrance of times past. So when
Did we win, and how? Apartheid, now dead
In Azania, lives in Palestine.
Therefore, look back in time, to look ahead:
We stickered tins of segregated fruit
In shops, and pressured banks to disinvest.
It was "not the destitute; prostitute,
But the man in the three-piece suit" that best
Explained support for a system of crime.

Humans cannot bear much reality,
Eliot wrote, as the Great Uprising
Against British Mandate Rule reached full swing.
(News unlikely to have strongly impinged
On literary walks *chez* Harrowby.)
Surely he was on to something cuter,
Though, when he added: "Time past and future
Point to one end." That's when freedom will win.
Let our own history be our tutor,
And we can all find Palestine within.

Notes and references

May 2023 saw commemorations for the 75th anniversary of Al Nakba, when hundreds of thousands of Palestinians were driven from their homes in a massive pre-planned act of ethnic cleansing at the formation of the State of Israel. It is still underway today, as attested by continued violence, at the hands of both officially sanctioned forces and armed extremists who enjoy near-total impunity, towards Palestinians in East Jerusalem.[14] The clear aim is to force them out.

I attended the demonstration against South African apartheid in Trafalgar Square in 1985—said then to be the largest ever in London, with at least half a million present. The speakers included the US civil rights leader, the Reverend Jesse Jackson. By that stage, the movement's focus had switched to calls for a global financial boycott—a point he emphasised with the dramatic words: "It is not the destitute; prostitute, but the man in the three-piece suit that is keeping apartheid alive in South Africa today!"

Later, when I was elected to be sabbatical Communications Officer at Cardiff University Student Union, we on the Exec made a small contribution by excluding Barclays Bank from the exhibitors at 'Freshers' Fayre'. The high street banks would prey on students wishing to open accounts to deposit their newly arrived grant cheques (how quaint!) While none of them was squeaky-clean, Barclays had distinguished itself by cultivating particularly close ties with South Africa and brazenly defending its actions. We kept the local branch manager fully informed of our decision and the reasons for it.

Fast-forward nearly forty years and, with credentialled opinion now unanimous that Israel is also committing the crime against humanity of apartheid, and governments reluctant to act, the onus is once again on building campaigns of boycott from the grassroots.

Spotter's corner: the Mahmoud Darwish poem referred to is *I Come From There*, with its poignant closing couplet: "I learnt all the words and broke them up/To make a single word: 'Homeland' …"

The remembrance of past times being prompted by coffee and madeleines refers to Marcel Proust's masterpiece, *A la recherche du temps perdu*. Its title is now usually rendered as 'In search of lost time', however for most of its life the English translation was the less accurate but more resonant *The Remembrance of Things Past*. The novel's legendary long narrative trains of recollection are touched off by dipping madeleines into coffee.

The TS Eliot quotes are from *Burnt Norton*, the first of his Four Quartets, included in *Collected Poems 1909–1935* (published 1936). The dates of the Great Uprising are usually given as 1936–39. Burnt Norton is a stately home in the Cotswolds where Eliot is said to have walked in the gardens—which then influenced the imagery of the poem. The house has been the country seat of the Lords Harrowby since 1753.

7. Assange Unbound

Bold Prometheus set the world aflame;
Revealing wrongs darker than death or night,
But caught on film, which drew unwanted fame
To inhumanity of shoot-on-sight;
Thus defied power, which seemed omnipotent
And, bound to rock, swore never to repent.

Swift Mercury, the messenger, would taunt:
"You too can be this free—if penitent."
But Titan heard echo in this détente
Of Master's Voice: concealed, yet dominant.
Such freedom comes at a ruinous price:
To yield to might, too great a sacrifice.

And hark! Deep music of the rolling world
Did reach the Lodge, with new red flag unfurled.
No bondage must stretch to infinite span,
Brave Albo quoth: 'tis Time, for a new plan.
So, with Jupiter due down from the skies,
Was the prisoner's face before all eyes.

A spirit from our hearts burst forth, and clad
In "Free Assange" raiment, of black and white
Would the Supreme confront, with calls for right
To Truth about Olympus, good or bad.
Till hope creates the thing it contemplate,
We'll ne'er forsake Julian to his fate.

O, Freedom! Long desired and long delayed!
Can light make antique empire insecure?
Or leaks expose the moral masquerade
Of 'goodies' and 'baddies' in every war?
Do they, in fact, make abundantly clear
That faith draws deep on hell's co-eval, fear?

How past leaders turned on one of our own!
Two-faced Janus from Marketing declared:
"Time to face the music," as though prepared
To say 'Aloha' without compunction.
Flame-haired Vesta, Gillard, was adamant
He'd performed offence against the Tyrant.

Will Jove grant pardon, seeking second term?
Might that depend on pressure we exert;
Lest ancient court proceed to extradite
And vengeful Grand Jury incriminate
To thus condemn Assange, to far-off date,
To suffer woes which Hope thinks infinite?

So pledge, as ye shiver in shirt of T
Neither to change, nor falter, nor recant
Till Good, great and joyous, is once more free,
And we may be informed participants
In all decisions taken in our name:
That alone would be worthy of thy fame!

Notes and references

Why is Julian Assange behind bars? The claim that WikiLeaks revelations endangered US personnel—put forward by prosecutors as the basis for demanding his extradition from the UK—is disingenuous and false. The trial of former Private Chelsea Manning, who supplied source material for the stories, heard from Brigadier General Robert Carr. In the witness box, he confirmed that an official US investigation had shown no deaths or injuries could be attributed as a result of the classified information being put into the public domain.

No—what is at stake is the ability to control the flow of information and the news agenda: seen as vital in securing public consent for continuing to wage wars of choice, which are, in turn, assessed as indispensable to US dominance.

Australian Prime Minister Anthony Albanese has positioned himself as sympathetic to calls for Assange to be released, saying that no purpose is served by his continuing incarceration—but that appears to be expected to 'stand in' for any use of his office or influence to actually do anything about it. At least that's better than his predecessor, Scotty from Marketing, whose 'Aloha' from office began with an ill-timed holiday on Hawai'i. Campaigners were planning to 'photo-bomb' President Joe "Jove" Biden on his scheduled visit to Sydney for Quad talks, all wearing 'Free Assange' T-shirts in the background (the visit was called off; the demo went ahead).

Spotter's corner: *Assange Unbound* borrows the style and meter of Percy Bysshe Shelley's *Prometheus Unbound*, a verse play that is seen as an exaltation of liberty, written and published in 1820 as England roiled with discontents under the unreformed repressive regime of the Georgian era. Shelley's text is, in turn, based on the play by Aeschylus that dramatizes the original Prometheus story: of the Titan god who stole fire from Olympus and gave it to humans, and was punished by being chained to a rock.

8. Greta and the garbos

Say 'Garbo' in some wealthy Sydney 'burb,
And you mean the movie star, right? Or wrong—
Since those wide streets would not look posh for long
If someone didn't pick up from the kerb.
Noonuccal notes an estate agent's sign,
Indicating where "rubbish may be tipped",
By some mansion, built across her song line.
Not to make this a complex manuscript—
Just, more of us now are feeling squeezed out,
Which may be what this struggle's all about.

'Workaround' could mean driving a bin-truck
The wrong way down a lane when no-one sees;
Or tax-cheat accountants pushing their luck
To prove money really does grow on trees.
If everyone was tightening their belts,
Essential servers might not feel the lack;
Instead they're watching as livelihood melts:
While profits soar, they're slipping further back.
To keep a roof above a family's head
Shouldn't mean skimping on their daily bread.

It's justice that nourishes the people,
Brecht declared, while breaking down the fourth wall
In theatre. When we see how something's made,
It can put us off, as with sausages.
We avert our eyes from the cavalcade
Of low-paid workers and their lossages
Who move daily past us, generally mute.
Now they've raised their voice, listen, and compute—
Could you live on 26 bucks an hour?
If not, let's support them, and empower.

"I just want to be alone," G Garbo
  Famously said. Not now—stand together,
And help them to land the decisive blow
  In dispute that feels like a bellwether:
Rogue bosses, trying to get clean away
With cutting overtime and rates of pay.
Plenty of others, looking for pretext
Will jump on this; so it could be you next.
Call on Sydney City to intervene,
So we all enjoy streets both fair and clean.

Notes and references

I was a garbo once, for a couple of months in 1988, after I finished my English degree, in the employment of Cardiff City Council. That was before the modern-day curse of 'out-sourcing'. Terms and conditions for public sector workers are seen as dispensable—to be lowered as far as possible in search of maximum profits. Cleanaway, the predatory outsourcing firm at the centre of the Sydney garbos' dispute of 2022–23, wanted to slash penalty rates paid for overtime, with the result that workers' take-home pay would stagnate or decrease amid a cost-of-living crisis.

Anger over these plans can only have increased with news that PwC, a global accountancy firm, had obtained details of forthcoming tax changes in a confidential budget briefing, and used them to help wealthy clients—mostly US tech companies—to devise 'workarounds' to minimise the tax they would pay. As an example of corporate greed amid public squalor, it could hardly better encapsulate the justice issues at the heart of the dispute. What appeared to add insult to injury was that PwC had been in the habit of scooping up lucrative outsourcing work itself—from the same federal government whose tax income it was conniving to reduce.

Spotter's corner: Bertolt Brecht's theatrical alienation techniques were calculated to let audiences in on the drama-making process, thereby prompting and equipping them to question what they were being shown and told. A habit we could all do with taking from the theatre into everyday life. "Justice is the bread of the people," he declared. "They need it every day." The Oodgeroo Noonuccal quote is from her famous poem, *We Are Going*.

9. Gadarene swine

The Gadarene herd ran off to their doom—
Thus proving we humans supreme.
No obligation should Christians assume,
To beings elsewhere in God's scheme.
Hence four-wheel-drives, when stampeding across
The Harbour Bridge from the North Shore,
Could not give a monkey's profit-and-loss:
Global warming, they can ignore.

So are they Christ's flock, or ill-fated swine,
These Porsches, Isuzus and Fords?
What part is theirs in this verse metaphor,
Now stretched like some posh limousine?
The miracle moved a demon inside
A man to 'inferior' beasts.
Feeling entitled? Your biblical guide:
Why have enough when you can feast?

Much more of that, and the earth will mutate,
Through increase of fumes, atmospheric.
So what can we do, to dodge the pigs' fate:
Presenting the data, numeric?
Or scraping a key down the paint on a door;
Might conscience be tricky to salve?
If you want to stay onside with the law,
Trap a lentil inside a valve.

All you'll be stealing is air from the tyre—
It seeps with a gradual hiss.
Just be elsewhere when the outcome transpires;
Reactions will not include bliss.
Improve public transport, working from home:
These notions will both serve us well.
Then we'll preserve our delicate biome
And together, all creatures may dwell.

Notes and references

If drivers of Sports Utility Vehicles were a nation, they would be the world's seventh-biggest emitter of greenhouse gases.[15] A marketing fad which has kept the car industry expanding arrived at just the point of the Anthropocene period—when human activity is the prime influence on the natural environment—when the rest of us could least afford it.

The Tyre Extinguishers have perfected a method for signalling the unacceptability of gas-guzzling vehicles, thundering along in urban areas, with lentils—thus immobilising them while committing no criminal offence.

"Deflating tyres repeatedly and encouraging others to do the same will turn the minor inconvenience of a flat tyre into a giant obstacle for driving massive killer vehicles around our streets," Marion Walker, a spokesperson for the group, told a sympathetic journalist.[16] "We're taking this action because governments and politicians have failed to protect us from these huge vehicles. Everyone hates them, apart from the people who drive them."

The miracle of the Gadarene swine was interpreted by theologians including St Thomas Aquinas as meaning that God was interested only in human souls, and the rest of creation could therefore be regarded as dispensable: an attitude that will eventually lead to our extinction, unless we disavow it.

10. Seeking asylum

Once a Johnny Howard went across to Washington
Under a Sheriff as Deputy;
And he sang as he saw smoke rising from the Pentagon,
Don't come a-seeking asylum with me!

Seeking asylum, seeking asylum
Don't come a-seeking asylum with me!
And he sang as he saw smoke rising from the Pentagon,
Don't come a-seeking asylum with me!

Back home to Canberra, speaking in the Parliament:
"We will decide who comes in the country!"
And he tricked, lied and cheated all the way to polling day,
Back with an increased majority.

Seeking asylum, seeking asylum
Don't come a-seeking asylum with me!
And he tricked, lied and cheated all the way to polling day,
Back with an increased majority.

Down came a poor boy, raised by a single mum,
Stopped Coalition terms, one-two-three;
And he sang as he looked at Little Johnny's policy,
"That one will do very nicely for me!"

Seeking asylum, seeking asylum
Don't come a-seeking asylum with me!
And he sang as he looked at Little Johnny's policy,
"That one will do very nicely for me!"

Up cut the ratbag, with smile that was satisfied:
"Just how secure is my legacy?"
And his ghost may be heard if you're passing close to Villawood:
Don't come a-seeking asylum with me!

Seeking asylum, seeking asylum
Don't come a-seeking asylum with me!
And his ghost may be heard if you're passing close to Villawood:
Don't come a-seeking asylum with me!

Notes and references

John Howard was in Washington—fulfilling the historic purpose of Australian Prime Ministers in going there, namely to receive their instructions—on 11 September 2001. He's reckoned as an eyewitness, since from his hotel window he could apparently see smoke rising from the attack on the Pentagon.

Barely a year before the electoral cycle would oblige him to seek a new mandate, Howard's government had languished, with polls showing a sustained Labor lead. Then, in the space of a fortnight, came two political windfalls. The first, in late August, saw a Norwegian freighter, the MV *Tampa*, turned away from Australian coastal waters when it was seeking safe haven for 438 Afghan refugees, rescued from a sinking wooden boat. The government rushed a new Border Protection Bill through parliament, with Howard declaring: "We will decide who comes to this country, and the circumstances in which they come."

Then, the Al Qaida attacks on New York and Washington handed the Coalition the opportunity to combine and conflate the supposed menace posed by people seeking refuge from persecution, with an amply demonstrated terrorist threat. A study by veteran editor-turned-researcher Peter Manning showed that, of newspaper articles published in Sydney in a two-year period after 9/11, of those referring to refugees or asylum-seekers, fully 37% also contained references to "terrorism".[17]

The effect exemplified Murray Edelman's concept of a "political spectacle": a form of control in which "aroused responses" are procured through a "mediated drama that objectifies hopes and fears",[18] usually by projecting bad feeling on to outsiders, thus allowing the author of the drama to divert attention away from less expedient issues.

Two decades on, is the policy under Anthony Albanese—the poor boy raised by a single mum—materially different? One of the most famous refugees held in detention under the previous Coalition ministry, the Iranian-Kurdish author and journalist, Behrooz Bouchani, has called it "inhumane, hypocritical, and a relic of the Liberals".[19]

Both and neither

1. Huskisson

How did William Huskisson perish?
Being unfamiliar with the train,
When one stopped (the water to replenish)
He stopped another—ending his campaign
Against the anti-slavery movement.
Captive humans must earn freedom, he wrote,
Through "moral and religious improvement"—
Rendering emancipation remote.

The engine that killed him was the Rocket,
Plying the world's first steam passenger route.
The impact pulled his leg from its socket,
And—prone, on a carriage door—he bled out.
News of his views came through an *exposé*,
After two centuries *absconditus*.
Progress literally swept him away,
In a rare case of poetic justice.

For a coastal town he's the eponym,
From his days in charge of the colonies.
Now history's caught up with just how grim
Those days were, surely that must cause unease?
A mere few decades have passed since the Mayor—
Who still fills a Council seat—set alight
An Aboriginal flag; taking care,
Of course, that a news camera was in sight.

Husky First Nations struggle to this day,
To keep their sacred burial site free
And covetous developers at bay.
It doubtless adds insult to injury
That land was handed over to the church,
Which sold it on for an apartment block.
Council listened, but left them in the lurch—
Giving no choice but to turn back the clock.

Back to protest smoking ceremony
To advocate for "basic human rights …
That speaks volumes to a community"
That believed it had stood and won those fights,
Charlie Ashby, a Jerrinja elder
Told a *New Bush Telegraph* reporter.
Things would be different if the ground held a
Trace of a European explorer.

In specialist report, experts averred
"High confidence" of fifty graves. The King
Of Jervis Bay, Bud Billy, is interred,
Local wisdom says. It means no building,
With due respect, should get the go-ahead.
So that's the decision, Australia:
Put culture before profit, or instead,
Doom reconciliation to failure.

Notes and references

There's a growing movement to replace colonial Australian place names. I am writing this from Sydney, or perhaps that should be Gadi, the Aboriginal name. But there's an extra, specific reason why people of the NSW South Coast should want to disavow their connection with William Huskisson, Colonial Secretary in the government of Lord Liverpool. He was killed in an accident when attending the official launch of the Liverpool-Manchester passenger railway, in 1830.

Huskisson stands unmasked by recent historical research as a prime mover in the campaign to delay and frustrate the abolition of slavery. The taking of slaves had already been outlawed. So at least the people of west Africa were no longer being snatched away from their homes at gunpoint and clapped in irons on British slave ships. But there was a fierce rearguard action by the 'West Indies Interest', owners of lucrative plantations and their allies back in Britain, to keep their unpaid labour force for as long as possible.

As a senior cabinet member, Huskisson posed as a neutral in the debate. But, in 1823, he showed his hand in a letter to John Gladstone, a politician and slave owner whose son, William, would later become Prime Minister in the Liberal cause. This confirmed the government was conniving to keep emancipation off the parliamentary agenda. And Huskisson coined what went on to become a key argument by 'the Interest': that slaves were just not ready for freedom. Not until they showed "moral and religious improvement ... by imperceptibly creating better domestic habits and feelings".

The letter made him a hero—to the slavers. Huskisson was described in a colonial newspaper, the *Dominica Chronicle*, as "the most important and useful member of the British legislature". This aspect of Huskisson's career does not appear in previous research about him, including his biography, published in the 1950s. The details are revealed by the historian, Michael Taylor, who went back to the original sources from two centuries ago.[20]

The naming of Huskisson has been taken up by an independent media project, the *New Bush Telegraph*. Its writers have also chronicled the campaign to keep greedy developers from building a block of holiday apartments on land surrounding the town's disused Anglican church, which independent surveys have shown is an Aboriginal burial site.[21] Still a leading figure in the pro-development lobby on the local Shoalhaven Council is Greg Watson, who as Mayor in the 1980s burned an Aboriginal flag for the benefit of a news photographer.[22] For the insight that Australia rhymes with failure, thank Phillip Adams.

2. The other side

To Sangkhlaburi's pagoda,
Wooden bridge across the Kwai;
First the planks in working order
Then begin to melt away.
"Stop looking down," our guide calls out,
Along the receding tide;
Reflect within and look without:
Shall we reach the other side?

When from their homes, in search of peace
To survive another day,
The people come as refugees
On the road from Mandalay—
Or rather by the jungle route,
From bullets they try to hide—
Reflect within and look without:
Shall they reach the other side?

She'd been a cook in far-off days
In renegade Kawthoolei;
Now caring for the emigrés
In shade of a banyan tree.
Her old Three Pagodas café—
Called 'Better Fed than Red'—
Abandoned as an epitaph
To beloved comrades, dead.

We'd brought her English medicines—
Rolled-up bandage, gauze and pins;
Blood pressure kit; a stethoscope;
Tubes of antiseptic soap.
They all looked up to the Lady
For a hope of future, bright;
Meanwhile, they'd come to our Daisy
To provide and set them right.

Gladdened by the reformation,
That latterly came to pass,
We'd recall our exploration
Of those dusty Shangri-las,
When the mist was on the rice-field
And the sun was dropping slow;
And hope for tyranny to yield;
Alas, it was not quite so.

Remember the jarring image
Of aerobics class online;
While trucks in dreary camouflage
Manoeuvre across behind?
Brutality in the background,
Too seldom recalled to mind.
Regime cracked down, and underground
Is dissension now confined.

We should have known it was coming,
Foreign Minister messed up:
Caught on mic reciting Kipling
Aloud, until told to stop.
Were his hosts ashamed to tell him
Of their country going wrong,
Thus reminded of days *passim*
Where the memories are long?

In Sangkhla, on our filming trip,
We prepared a focus-rack:
Burmese discussing exileship
While ants hurried forth and back;
One far away from camera-lens—
The contrasting, close beside.
So look without, reflect within:
Shall they reach the other side?

Now exiles form a government;
Come requesting our support;
Not bandages, beside the point—
Just make sure we don't consort
With dictators and criminals
Who squat in power and loot;
Instead, give them the wherewithal
Of a three-fingered salute.

The world, if warned, will look around
And waggle its head in woe;
But what about the old background—
Is that where this woe will go?
We are the world, without a doubt,
We can turn about that tide;
Reflect within and look without:
Let's all reach the other side.

Notes and references

Over 20 years ago now, a visit to Sangkhlaburi in western Thailand took me to a community of Burmese exiles, forced out by the military when the Karen National Liberation Army stronghold, free Kawthoolei, was overrun. Trapped as illegal immigrants, they were in need of support, which we brought in the form of medical aid. The other purpose of the trip was to document their plight and their dreams of a brighter future. Pictures appeared on the UK Sky News, in two feature pieces that aired some months later, and an account was published in the *Independent*. It featured Daisy Dooe, who had run a restaurant in the town of Three Pagodas but was now operating as an independent aid worker.[23]

Today, their predicament is shared anew, as Burma's peoples flee the military dictatorship that crushed their nascent democracy in a coup d'état in 2021. Extraordinarily, the seizure of power was captured on video in the background of an online aerobics class in Naypyidaw, with the teacher, facing the camera of course, oblivious to the troop movements behind her. The writing was inspired by a visit to the University of Sydney (on 2 June 2023) by Aung Myo Min, Human Rights Minister in the National Unity Government, to receive a Gold Medal for his human rights work from the Sydney Peace Foundation.

Spotter's corner: By far the best-known English poem about Burma is Rudyard Kipling's *Mandalay*, generally accounted a technically brilliant piece of verse which is also, in most critics' eyes, a paean to British imperialism. It surfaced in the news a few years ago, when Boris Johnson was the UK's Foreign Minister, and was recorded by a camera crew reciting it aloud during a visit to Yangon. The British Ambassador could be heard shushing him: "Not appropriate, Minister!"

It evidently retains a certain grip on Anglophone images of the country, so I am trying to make my own small contribution to loosening it. Hence *The Other Side* adopts the same rhythm and meter, and (mis)quotes one or two Kipling lines. For instance, instead of "the road to Mandalay", we now have "the road *from* Mandalay", seeming to capture the intended feeling of reversal in key messages, compared with the original.

Old Sod

1. Snapshots of Brexit

I. Normandy, July 2017

On *vacances en famille* to Normandy
In jolly *gîte au joli paysage*,
The in-laws shunned the Bayeux Tapestry.
These prudent English folk *d'un certain age*
Had watched it, *ils declaraient*, on TV;
And anyway, who would pay to see that?
A *claque* of French conquerors, showing off,
And our man with an arrow in his hat?
Whole thing's as rotten as a *mauvais oeuf*.

But the beaches? *Maintenant* you're talking:
You've monuments to good brave boys and true,
And spanking *nouveau* visitor centre
With toilet genders limited to two.
Summon up the image, while you're walking,
Of that famous wartime cartoon by Low,
Showing Tommy as a lone dissenter.
Fancy yourself in an Allied landing;
Enjoy the vicarious afterglow.

Border checks hardly slowed our momentum.
We enjoyed free movement in the EU.
This, just a year past the referendum,
Before the rules were all drawn up anew.
Rights would surely never turn to vapour?
Continentals would have to play our game.
This they knew, they'd read it in the paper—
We'd keep our market access just the same.
If not, we'd simply go to court, and sue.

We, *de l'autre côté*, sounded naïve,
Saying "Don't blame us—we voted Remain".
After all, no-one could really believe
That any lasting damage would pertain.
So now, we enjoy our sovereign right
To flush our export business down the drain.
That's one reason to carry on the fight.
Then, there's the point of who we really are:
Mere faded empire, or twenty-eighth star?

II. Yorkshire, November 2019

Seeking 'vox pops', before election day
At the Brontë Parsonage Museum—
The fields behind, with friendly dog at play
And determined owner, seventy-eight.
"Being bossed about by Europeans",
And her keenness, such to repudiate,
Meant she'd back a Leave-inclined candidate—
With passion reminiscent of Jane Eyre—
When she came, among parties, to compare.

How quintessentially English a scene!
Pale winter sun dappled the Yorkstone walls,
With rival-coloured posters in between.
Brontë *père* sent his daughter, you'll recall,
To Brussels. Today, they'd all have a claim
To EU passports, through his Irish birth,
As 'O'Prunty', their original name.
Just think of the blessings that might be worth,
Compared with being stuck down memory lane.

Ireland now is better off than Britain;
Poland and Slovenia soon as well.
At least we've got our cultural glories:
Some of the finest words ever written.
Even ruling out the Brontë stories,
That Shakespeare connection is ours to sell.
His settings? In Denmark, you'll need Kroner,
And Euros for Athens or Verona.
On that, perhaps, it's impolite to dwell …

III. Wiltshire, October 2020

What did the Romans ever do for us?
An outdoor mosaic at Littlecote House
Depicts Orpheus, charming with his lyre.
Sweep back fallen leaves, to show the seasons:
Grain goddess Demeter's one to admire.
An Elizabethan red-brick mansion
With arboretum creates more reasons
To visit in search of mind expansion,
On the Downs of North Wessex (that's Wiltshire).

Life at the ancient villa overlapped
With the migration period, when folk
Of *Pax Romana* were forced to adapt
As 'barbarians' overran their homes.
To honour mixed heritage now is 'woke',
Apparently: but slaves who cleaned the stones,
Even worshippers at the pagan shrine,
Must occasionally have crossed the line
With locals they were eager to uncloak.

Henry the Eighth came courting here, it's said,
And William of Orange later stayed
At the house, on his way to claim the throne:
The second King Billy we imported.
When you hear, "We'll do better on our own,"
Remember we've a gene pool assorted
By comings and goings since time of yore.
Leaving was not supposed to make us poor,
So how can Brexit now be overthrown?

"Only connect," Forster wrote, in his tale
Of Schlegel sisters—half-German, clever—
And Wilcoxes, classic spoilt English males,
Whose "criminally muddled" endeavours
Ruined others' lives, while oblivious.
Plus ça change! So, point out the obvious:
Der Tumult is of our fabrication.
Above all, recognise, and be joyous:
We're bred as a European nation.

Notes and references

Basil Fawlty—played by the imperishable John Cleese—at one point in his erratic career as a hotelier, storms out over some irreconcilable dilemma, only to discover it's raining. He looks up at the sky, registers how cold and inhospitable it is on the outside, turns on his heel (in that inimitable Basilic manner), then presents himself to Sybil at reception and tries to book into Fawlty Towers as a guest. Britain has not quite reached that stage—not yet.

In *Snapshots of Brexit*, I look deeper into who the Brexit British think they are, and where they think they came from, seeking explanations for why so many supported a proposal to detach them from their own continent when that was so clearly inimical to their interests. That famous cartoon by David Low, in the London *Evening Standard* from June 1940, shows a menacing sky full of Nazi warplanes and the foreground figure exclaiming, "Very well—alone!" Such notions doubtless exert all too strong an influence.

The vox pops at the Brontë museum came on a reporting assignment for *Byline Times*, an excellent independent media outlet,[24] while gathering material for a constituency profile of perennially marginal Keighley (which did indeed change hands in 2019 from Labour to Tory).

The message is slowly getting through, with a sustained and rising majority telling pollsters they now believe Brexit was a mistake. But none of the main political parties will enter the next General Election (expected, at time of writing, within a year or so) committed to renewing British membership. It might be left to the tiny Rejoin EU Party[25] to grow by steady accretion, to the point where the main parties start to lose enough votes to miss out on target seats, before it returns to the agenda.

Spotter's corner: in EM Forster's novel, *Howards End*, Margaret Schlegel's near-superhuman forbearance eventually runs out and she scolds the wealthy businessman, Henry Wilcox, for his double standards: "You are muddled, Henry! Criminally muddled!"

2. Britain in 2023

An old, mad, blind, despised and dying sect;
Ministers, dregs with muddled minds, who sow
Division through invective wild and flecked
With foam of fury aimed at those below;
Rulers who from cold science know too well
That fossil fuels released from ocean's grasp
Must surely pave the road to earthly hell,
But leechlike to polluting donors clasp.
Police, whom liberticide of protest
Makes tyrannic, by statute harsh and mean;
Politics witless—a gutless contest
For unprincipled voters in between—
Are waves on which a Rebellion may
Ride, to power with sun's light our darkest day.

Notes and references

This is an updated version of Shelley's righteously angry sonnet, *England in 1819*, written in response to the Peterloo massacre, in which protestors for political rights were attacked by army troops. Today's equivalent liberticidal tendencies were on display when police implemented new anti-protest laws by arresting and locking up republicans, at the Coronation of Charles III, simply for carrying placards saying, "Not my King".

Such is the routinised corruption of Rishi Sunak's Conservative government that these violations of civil liberties were rammed through parliament after being devised and proposed by a corporate-funded think-tank, Policy Exchange, which has a direct line to ministers. Among its sponsors is the oil giant, ExxonMobil, and the original target of the clampdown was Extinction Rebellion[26]—hence the reference in the poem. The campaign group has significant achievements to its credit, making it a threat to the fossil fuel industry.[27] The whims of the latter are translated straight into policy without the bat of an eyelid.

Tory MPs in far-from-negligible numbers are continually trying to downgrade global heating from an accepted scientific fact to a mere 'theory', implying there is some doubt or room for debate over it. In Commons Questions to the Climate Minister, Southport's Damien Moore asked: "What scientific evidence his department has which demonstrates the need to reduce the amount of carbon dioxide in the atmosphere?" Yes still, in 2023. The monitoring website, They Work For You, notes that "Damien Moore generally voted against measures to prevent climate change".[28]

3. Getting to Yes in Wales

In the shallows of Cwm-yr-Eglwys bay,
We watched some hungry mackerel on the hunt.
The tiny village nestled on the way
To a vertiginous stretch of seafront.
But residents have dwindled down to two,
As houses get snapped up for second homes,
Like the whitebait we saw from our canoe.
It is in Wales; just not where Welsh folk come.

A Principality must have its Prince:
A fresh one, with all due pomp invested.
How chose he, this loyalty to evince?
Visiting a sports event contested
Between his fiefdom and her 'big brother'.
To show support for Gareth and the boys?
No—he'd come to wish luck on the other:
The kind of thing that rankles and annoys.

So no wonder Yes Cymru is booming:
The glory days of home rule may be nigh.
Dragons, colour of spilled blood, are looming
From banners held aloft in the wild sky;
Here's no present, didn't that poet say—
Only past (and never mind the future)?
So how come the demo's on *Wales Today*?
Hope for change must be the best recruiter.

Maybe that's too literal and too linear.
Never be lucid, or directly state
The simplest thought, for verse to pass the ear
Of modern readers, Dylan would relate.
So hear it in puffins' growls on Skomer,
Or stopping-service klaxon, running late.
Sniff it in Port Talbot's dank aroma
Or SA, Brains' ambrosia, potate.

Digging in beside a fellow worker,
Tremorfa's furnace stopped a fortnight cool:
The one, a student, though not a shirker;
His comrade, a skilled man played for a fool.
Wage packets for toilers like my neighbour
Once arrived with British Steel guarantee.
Where to now, the profits from their labour?
Across the bible-black, boat-bobbing sea.

'The union' used to be the cow's head,
A thing the prudent person kept in sight.
Could it be, today, the bull's tail instead,
Next to the bit where you don't shine a light?
Not to mention surpluses, of power,
Food, water, sent away for others' gain;
Or the language, nation's heart and flower,
Of which just *Croeso*—welcome—need pertain.

Notes and references

Wales has never voted Tory, yet its people have suffered at the sharp end of Tory policies that have wrenched apart the haves and have-nots in every corner of Britain. The benefits of union with England used to be evident in jobs with the National Coal Board and British Steel. During the year-long strike to stave off pit closures, we student activists visited picket lines, and rattled buckets at the entrance to the union building for donations to the hardship fund. But it was lost, devastating mining communities for generations.

By the time I got vacation work as a casual labourer during 'stop fortnight' at Cardiff's Tremorfa steel works, we were rubbing shoulders with men whose industry was at risk of following coal into oblivion. The biggest remnant of steel in Wales is the Port Talbot plant: now owned by the Indian conglomerate, Tata, with a small fraction of its former workforce (though its legendary pong is apparently just as strong).

The last Welsh Prince of Wales was Llewellyn ap Gruffudd, in the 13th Century. The new one, William, marked his accession with a fan visit to the England football team before their departure for the World Cup in Qatar. Their group-stage opponents included, yes, Wales, under legendary captain Gareth Bale.

Yes Cymru is Britain's fastest-growing political movement. Pollsters now find independence supported by over a third of respondents, up from single figures just a few years ago. Seeing billions spent on rail investment in England, while Wales' own network is a byword for decrepitude, has contributed. As a mere *Saesneg*, having returned many times to Wales, I have never felt anything other than warmly welcomed.

Spotter's corner: Dylan Thomas inveighs against excessive lucidity in modern verse to his Aunt, of course. The "bible-black, fishing-boat-bobbing sea" is from his play for voices, *Under Milkwood*. And RS Thomas, in *A Welsh Landscape*, saw Wales as having neither present nor future, only past. *Wales Today* is the name of the BBC's English-language evening television news programme. The references to the cow's head and bull's tail are from a popular Welsh language saying, *Gwell gweld pen buwch na chynffon tarw*; meaning, it's reckoned, "Better to see what you can trust than what you can't."[29]

4. Lab or a Tory?

Only a few can understand
Differences 'twixt Rishi and Keir;
To Tory dogmas, by command
His Labour Party must adhere.

Only a few may comprehend
What Brexit means o'er there or here:
A policy they won't amend
For fear of Farage up the rear.

Few indeed can discriminate
Civil rights in one from t'other:
Protestors have learned to conflate
People's party with Big Brother.

And very few can clearly get
How to tell Lab from Tory shit:
Water, still a private asset,
To no hygienic benefit.

All topics of political chatter,
Where it is, of course, the few that matter.

Test it in a laboratory:
Lab or a Tory, which would you be?
You sound surprised at the result:
Building houses on the green belt.

Politer language; sober suits;
Less conspicuous culture war;
You must see these would be the fruits
Of throwing scoundrels out the door.

Else there's really no hope for you
When analysing politics;
Not a good idea to bore you
With finer points of pollsters' tricks.

Hope for change? You'll have a long wait.
That's democracy for you, mate.

Notes and references

Dampening down expectations ahead of an anticipated election victory is second nature to a social democratic party, and has been observed in countless cases—including Boundless Plains and Old Sod alike. Labour under Keir Starmer does seem to have an unerring knack of striking rigid positions that then put it on the wrong side of evolving public opinion, however. As noted above, Britons' realisation of how they were scammed over Brexit has hardened appreciably since he committed the party to "make it work" (free advice: it won't).

A previous pledge to renationalise the water industry was dropped, just as outrage erupted over rivers of shit—raw sewage being pumped out via watercourses into bathing waters, now blissfully free of EU regulations on quality, while the bonanza of dividends to shareholders and bonuses to executives continues. And Labour has gone through the motions of opposing Tory depredations on the right to protest, while undermining efforts by others to impede the passage of relevant legislation.[30] It proposes to solve the housing crisis by giving developers what they have wanted for decades, namely building access on land designated, in iconic legislation of the early post-war years, as 'green belt'.

5. Ode: Intimations of Inveracity from Recollections of Labour Childhood

There was a time when I rolled down a hill
And crashed into a startled dog.
Quickly, goodwill
Returned when, through the Hampstead fog,
We recognised the owner from his Bill
In Parliament, as those steep fields are named:
Michael Foot, then tyro—
Even hero—
Before the leader's role, for which he's lately famed;
'Dizzy' was the creature's appellation—
From Disraeli, patron of 'one nation'.

Beauty of Foot's Employment Act!
Safeguards from being sacked
And pay for pregnant mums
Wreathed with celestial light our confidence
That basic minimums
Of sex equivalence
And such the like
Would be attained, at least in childbirth.
But Labour lost and needs must take a hike,
And there had passed a dream of glory from the earth.

While darkness fell, it never stilled our song.
But when the bosses' greed
Infringed on human need,
To some of us there came a thought of grief.
A timely resolution brought relief,
And we again were strong:
Class tribunes blew their trumpets from the deep;
No more would grief of mine the struggle wrong;
We heard the echoes through the unions throng:
Colliers would alive the old flame keep,
As they had done before.
Coal and sweat
Of pickets, closing Saltley's gate
Had stopped Heath's unjust law
Back in 'seventy-two, and 'four.
So surely now?
But victor's laurels ne'er would sit upon King Arthur's brow.

So made anew was party, platform, all:
Give up on turning back the clock!
Accept, and grow the voting bloc!
My heart was at your festival,
My head had its coronal,
The fullness of your bliss, I felt—I felt it all.
Oh evil day! if I were sniping
While Earth herself was adorning
That sweet May-morning;
And journalists were typing
On every side,
In a thousand columns far and wide,
Fresh plaudits; while the sun shone warm,
And the Babe leapt up on his Mother's arm:
I heard, I heard, with joy I heard!
But there's a sedge, of many, one,
In single field which I have looked upon,
That spoke to me of something that was gone.
Campaign-ers by my side
Did the same tale provide:
Whither was fled the visionary gleam?
Where was it now, the glory and the dream?

Five pledges on a card the programme set:
Youth off benefits, into work at last;
Track punishment for young offenders fast,
Were two, lest we forget.
Shades of the prison-house began to close
Upon the growing boy
(Or girl) who must behold the light, and joy,
Their talents to impose.
Not in entire forgetfulness,
And not in utter nakedness,
But trailing clouds of glory Progress came …
To stick with Tory budget just the same;
And by the vision splendid
Was on its way attended.
Joining Europe's currency overruled,
And calls for public railways ridiculed;
At length the voters saw it die away,
And fade into the light of common day.

Hastened by chief warmonger, Tone,
As pre-conceived plot began to unwind,
Yearnings to follow, of unnatural kind,
And most unworthy aim.
The old UN did all it could
To set and follow rules for common good;
Forget Donald's unknowns, unknown
And that imperial palace whence he came.

Behold the boy among his new-found bliss,
Who cut the elder brother down to size!
See where, 'mid work of his own hand he lies,
To carve in stone every heartfelt promise.
Then, at his feet, some little chart or plan,
Some fragment from his dream of human life,
Shaped by himself, with SPADs in caravan
And dialogue with business, dodging strife.
Mugs controlling immigration;
A freeze on corporate tax rates;
Repeal health privatisation;
Technical Baccalaureates.
And this now hath his heart,
But it will not be long
Ere this be thrown aside,
And with new joy and pride
The little Actor cons another part;
Filling from time to time his 'humorous stage',
As bacon sandwich fails to fit his tongue;
Equanimity melting down to rage,
And Tory win from Lib Dem camouflage;
As if his whole vocation
Were contrite lamentation.

Then thou, whose outer semblance doth belie
Wardrobe's extensity;
Thou best philosopher, who yet dost keep
Artisan bread and hummus in the fridge;
That, Left and righteous, slumbered Bennite sleep,
Until aroused to slay Oxbridge
In leadership contest.
Mighty Prophet! Seer blest!
On whom those truths do rest.
Assailed by thine internal enemies;
In darkness lost, outside of the EU;
Thou, over whom the nineteen-seventies
Brood still today, as though still shiny-new—
A Presence which is all too close at hand.
Bearded Wonder! Inclined perhaps to stand
With support from Momentum Refounded;
Why with such earnest pains dost thou provoke
The years to bring the inevitable joke,
Leaving chroniclers astounded:
That members were so many under you,
Then after—thy blessedness past—so few?

O joy! That in the embers
Was something Left over;
Yet convincing those remaining members
Would prove no pushover!
Thought of cherished policies drew from Keir
An undertaking not to oversteer;
So they voted gaily
Against his rival, who was wrong, daily.
But new-fledged hope with disappointment met;
Not for him I raise
The song of thanks and praise
But for obstinate questionings
On past commitments he'd rather forget:
Once so solid on Palestine,
Then denying apartheid's threat;
Once keen on public stakeholdings,
Now regulation is the line.
Yet still those first affections,
Or shadowy recollections,
Are truths that wake, to perish never:
Neither listlessness, nor mad endeavour
Can finally abolish or destroy
Common dreams of a world compatible with joy.

Then sing, ye birds, Wordsworth exhorted, sing!
As former dinosaurs, wouldn't they know,
Somewhere too deep for tears,
What mass extinction brings?
So let the young Lambs bound,
Even Ministers' hounds:
We will cheer with gusto
Any who feel the gladness of the May.
In years that bring the philosophic mind,
Let human impulse never fall behind:
Allow its tenderness, its joys, and fears
To counsel everything we do and say.
Radiate to all living things:
Preserve the meadows, groves and hills;
The brooks, now bubbling brown with sewage spills.
The clouds that gather round the setting sun
Protect us from the radiance all too bright;
So tax, tax that oil and gas extraction
Before the dying of the light!
O, jaundiced eye,
Which hath watched o'er Labour's mortality
Through decades past;
Pray lead us, at the last,
To voting system of proportionality;
Another race will be, and palms be won:
Then new-born Day will dawn, for everyone.

Notes and references

I would have been eight years old, enjoying a springtime family walk on Hampstead Heath, when I rolled down the grassy slope of Parliament Hill Fields and collided with a small dog. It turned out to belong to Michael Foot, then Employment Minister in the newly elected Labour government and a leading figure of the Left, who lived nearby.

The preceding Conservative ministry of Ted Heath hit trouble when miners won their industrial dispute of 1972 by mobilising thousands of 'flying pickets' to close a coking plant at Saltley, near Birmingham. They triumphed again in '74, but their year-long strike led by Arthur Scargill, a decade later—not over pay this time, but to save their industry—could not repeat the trick.

William Wordsworth's Pindaric ode, *Intimations of Immortality from Recollections of Early Childhood*, is reckoned as a hymn to humans' essential goodness and kindness, which can be perceived even through the battering they endure in life and the distortions it can produce in their sensibilities and behaviours. Faith in those qualities is surely indispensable to any form of democratic Left politics, if only to sustain hope through such ups and downs as experienced by UK Labour over the past half-century or so.

Its high point electorally came in the guise of New Labour, whose appeal was more notable for its breadth than depth, and whose moral authority under Tony Blair (Lab, Sedgefield) dribbled away into the sands of Iraq. Ed Miliband then surprisingly snatched the leadership from his elder brother, David. His promises were (literally) carved on a stone, though it looked suspiciously as if made of polystyrene; his "controlling immigration" mugs are now collector's items, and his geekish unsuitability for office was apparently confirmed by his inelegant consumption, before news cameras, of a bacon sandwich. The verses on Jeremy Corbyn and Keir Starmer bring us up to date.

Notes

1. Terence Hawkes, 'Swisser-Swatter: making a man of English letters', in *Alternative Shakespeares*, ed John Drakakis. New York: Routledge, 1985, p 46.
2. Georgia Brown, *Hello*: 'Ten times royal ladies have broken fashion protocol with their outfits', 8 July 2021: <https://www.hellomagazine.com/fashion/royal-style/20210708117104/royal-ladies-breaking-royal-fashion-protocol/>
3. Millie Costigan, *Canberra Times*: 'Australian earl very excited at his role in coronation of Charles III', 5 May 2023: <https://www.canberratimes.com.au/story/8175476/aussie-earl-very-excited-for-his-role-in-the-coronation/>
4. Matilda Boseley, *Guardian*: 'Prince Charles' letter to John Kerr reportedly endorsing sacking of Whitlam condemned', 24 October 2020: <https://www.theguardian.com/uk-news/2020/oct/24/prince-charless-letter-to-john-kerr-reportedly-endorsing-sacking-of-whitlam-condemned>
5. Alison Broinowski, 'Australia prepares legal case for war over "non-sovereign nation" Taiwan', *Pearls and Irritations*, 12 April 2023: <https://johnmenadue.com/australia-prepares-legal-case-for-war-over-non-sovereign-nation-taiwan/>
6. Andrew Taylor, *The King's Evil*. London: Harper Collins, 2019.
7. Anne Pender, *The Conversation*: 'Remembering Barry Humphries, the man who enriched the culture, reimagined the one man show and upended the cultural cringe', 22 April 2023: <https://theconversation.com/remembering-barry-humphries-the-man-who-enriched-the-culture-reimagined-the-one-man-show-and-upended-the-cultural-cringe-188719>
8. Jordyn Beazley and Australian Associated Press, *Guardian*: 'Climate activist Deanna 'Violet' Coco's 15-month jail sentence quashed on appeal', 15 March 2023: <https://www.theguardian.com/australia-news/2023/mar/15/climate-activist-deanna-violet-cocos-15-month-jail-sentence-overturned-on-appeal>
9. For the full story: <https://www.edo.org.au/meet-the-two-climate-impacted-knitting-nannas-using-the-law-to-protect-our-democratic-freedoms-in-nsw/>
10. For the full story: <https://www.thedogonthetuckerbox.com/poemsfolk_songs>
11. Rachel Evans, *Green Left Weekly*: 'Traditional owners demand Empire Energy stop plans to frack Beetaloo Basin', 1 June 2023: <https://www.greenleft.org.au/content/traditional-owners-demand-empire-energy-stop-plans-frack-beetaloo-basin>
12. Alison Broinowski, 'Australia prepares legal case for war over "non-sovereign nation" Taiwan', *Pearls and Irritations*, 12 April 2023: <https://johnmenadue.com/australia-prepares-legal-case-for-war-over-non-sovereign-nation-taiwan/>

13 Marilyn Lake, 'From Yellow Peril to Red Alert', *Pearls and Irritations*, 17 March 2023: <https://johnmenadue.com/from-yellow-peril-to-red-alert/>
14 Amnesty International, 'Second night of horror at Al-Aqsa Mosque', 11 April 2023: <https://www.amnesty.org.au/second-night-of-horror-at-al-aqsa-mosque/>
15 Niko Kommenda, 'SUVs second biggest cause of emissions rise, figures reveal', Guardian, 25 October 2019: <https://www.theguardian.com/environment/ng-interactive/2019/oct/25/suvs-second-biggest-cause-of-emissions-rise-figures-reveal>
16 Willow Shah-Neville, '"By the time anyone wakes up, the tyre is fully deflated"/The emerging climate group using lentils to 'disarm' SUVs', Pulse Pod: <https://pulsepod.globalpulses.com/pod-feed/post/by-the-time-anyone-wakes-up-the-tyre-is-fully-deflated-the-emerging-climate-group-using-lentils-to-disarm-suvs>
17 Peter Manning, *Dog-Whistle Politics and Journalism*. Sydney: Australian Centre for Independent Journalism, 2004.
18 Murray Edelman, *Constructing the Political Spectacle*. Chicago: University of Chicago Press, 1988, p 91.
19 Behrooz Bouchani, 'Labor's refugee treatment is inhumane, hypocritical and a relic of the Liberals', *Crikey*, 22 March 2023: <https://www.crikey.com.au/2023/03/22/behrouz-boochani-labor-refugee-nauru-port-moresby/>
20 Michael Taylor, *The Interest: How the British Establishment Resisted the Abolition of Slavery*. London: Penguin, 2020.
21 Bonnie Cassen, 'Can the Huskisson Church still be saved?', *New Bush Telegraph*, 25 August 2021: <https://newbushtelegraph.org.au/can-the-huskisson-church-still-be-saved/>
22 Preserved for posterity by the Huskisson Heritage Association: <https://huskissonheritage.com.au/the-burning-of-the-aboriginal-flag-by-mayor-greg-watson-july-1982/>
23 Jake Lynch, 'Week in the Life: Daisy Dooe, Aid Worker, Thailand: Easing the pain of exiles' life in Limbo', *Independent*, 6 March 1999: <https://www.independent.co.uk/news/week-in-the-life-daisy-dooe-aid-worker-thailand-easing-the-pain-of-exiles-life-in-limbo-1078704.html>
24 Jake Lynch, 'Keighley: Could Rail Re-nationalisation Stop the Conservative Party in its Tracks?' *Byline Times*, 18 November 2019: <https://bylinetimes.com/2019/11/18/keighley-could-rail-re-nationalisation-stop-the-conservative-party-in-its-tracks/>
25 Rejoin EU: The only future for our generation: <https://therejoineuparty.com/>
26 Adam Bychawski, 'Revealed: Policing Bill was dreamed up by secretive oil-funded think tank', *Open Democracy*, 15 June 2022: <https://www.opendemocracy.net/en/dark-money-investigations/policing-bill-policy-exchange-exxonmobil-lobbying/>

27. Louise Boyle, 'As Extinction Rebellion pauses disruptive tactics, what have its climate protests achieved?', *Independent*, 26 January 2023: <https://www.independent.co.uk/climate-change/news/extinction-rebellion-protest-activism-oil-b2264618.html>
28. They Work For You: Damien Moore, Conservative MP for Southport: <https://www.theyworkforyou.com/mp/25630/damien_moore/southport/divisions?policy=1030>
29. Steffan Rhys, '18 spectacular Welsh sayings that will make you say "How the hell did we think of that?"', *Wales Online*, 26 November 2020: <https://www.walesonline.co.uk/lifestyle/fun-stuff/18-spectacular-welsh-sayings-make-19349992>
30. Josiah Mortimer, *Byline Times*, 'Anger as Labour refuses to back bid to stop government quietly changing definition of disruptive protest', 8 June 2023: <https://bylinetimes.com/2023/06/08/anger-as-labour-refuses-to-back-bid-to-stop-government-quietly-changing-definition-of-disruptive-protest/>

www.ingramcontent.com/pod-product-compliance
Lightning Source LLC
Chambersburg PA
CBHW020329010526
44107CB00054B/2036